George Washington

by Clara Ingram Judson

Illustrated by Bob Patterson

jB
W 277ju

Follett Publishing Company

Chicago

Library of Congress Catalog Card Number: 61-8805
© 1961, by Follett Publishing Company
Manufactured in the United States of America
Published simultaneously in Canada
by The Ryerson Press, Toronto

123456789

When George Washington was a boy, he lived on a farm in Virginia. His father had pigs and cows, geese and chickens. He had horses too.

George liked the horses best. He had his own pony, Whitefoot.

George was always a good rider. He liked to ride his pony over the fields.

Some days he rode Whitefoot to school.
The school was in a little cabin on the farm.

Later George went to a better school.
There he learned more about writing and
arithmetic.

But George Washington did not go
to school very much. He learned about
horses and farming from his father and his
brothers.

He learned good manners from watching
people.

When George was eleven years old, his
father died. After that George often stayed at
Mount Vernon, the home of his brother Lawrence.

George liked Lawrence's home. There were
always parties and friends at Mount Vernon.

George was a tall, strong, good-looking
boy. Lawrence's friends liked George.
They treated him like a man.

One day when George was at his mother's
home, he found some tools and a long chain.

"Those are your father's surveying tools,"
his mother said. "Your father was a surveyor."

"What is a surveyor?" George asked.

"He is a man who measures land. When
people buy farms, the land must be surveyed so
they will know where the farm begins and ends."

Maybe I can be a surveyor, George thought.

When he was nearly fifteen, George went
to see a surveyor in town.

"I would like to be a surveyor, sir,"
he said. "Will you teach me?"

"It is hard work," the man said. "I walk
for miles and work in the rain and cold and mud."

"I could carry your tools, sir," George said.
"And I can make maps."

"Come in," the surveyor said. He needed
a boy who could make maps.

So George began to learn to be a surveyor.

When George was sixteen years old, he went on a long trip with a surveying party. They had to measure wilderness land that belonged to one of Lawrence's friends.

On that trip George learned about living in the wilderness. He slept in a tent or under the stars. He shot wild turkeys and cooked the meat over a fire.

The surveying party often saw trappers and traders. One night an Indian war party camped near the surveyors.

George had a little book. In it he wrote down what he saw on the trip. He wrote about the Indians' war dance:

"They clear a large circle and make a great fire in the middle. Then they sit around it. A speaker tells them how they are to dance. The best dancer jumps up and runs and jumps about the ring. The rest then begin..."

In the next year George learned more
about surveying. When he was not working,
he often stayed at the home of a cousin.

George had a good time hunting and
playing games with his cousins. Everyone
liked George, and they liked to hear about
his trips.

One day when George was at Mount Vernon, Lawrence said to him:

"I hear that a surveyor is needed in the next county. You must pass a test to get the job. I think you can pass it."

George rode a long way to take that test. He passed it and got the job.

He was just seventeen years old. He had a man's job. Lawrence was proud of his brother.

George was now over six feet tall and very big and strong. No one could ride a horse better than he could. Men liked him and trusted him. He was a born leader.

As he did his surveying, George learned
more and more about his country, its big
rivers and rich lands. He learned to love
it more and more. He thought he would
like to serve his country.

When he was twenty-one years old, George
Washington became a major in the Virginia army.

He was still a surveyor too and still took long trips into the wilderness.

Some nights he stayed at places where traders and trappers were staying. Often they talked as they sat around the fire.

One night a trader said, "I hear the French are coming down from Canada."

"Yes," a trapper said. "The Indians are with them. They're building a fort way up near Lake Erie."

George had heard about the fort from other traders. He knew it would mean trouble between England and France.

At that time, Virginia and the other American colonies belonged to England. The English king sent a governor to rule each of his colonies.

In Europe, England and France were nearly always at war. Both countries claimed land in America.

Then George heard that the king had ordered the governor of Virginia to tell the French to get out. But who would take the message?

The French fort near Lake Erie was very far away. George had never gone so far. But he liked adventure, and he wanted to serve his country.

George went to the governor of Virginia.

He said, "I will take your message to the French."

Some other men and an Indian guide went with George. The trip was long and very hard. It was in winter, and very cold. But they got to the French fort.

When he got back to Virginia, George
said to the governor, "The French will
not go. They mean to build more forts.
They are making friends of the Indians."

"We will make them go,"
said the governor.

Soon after that, war began. Soldiers
from England and from the colonies fought
to drive out the French and Indians.

After seven years the war was over.
The English won. They kept all their
American colonies and took Canada from the
French.

When the war was over, George Washington
was a colonel. He had led the soldiers of
the Virginia colony.

Now he could stop being a soldier. He
could go back to Mount Vernon. Lawrence
had died, and Mount Vernon belonged
to George.

George added new rooms to the house and sent to England for new furnishings. Then he married Martha Custis.

A busy, happy time now began for George Washington. Day after day he rode out over his farms. He made plans for plowing, planting, and harvesting.

He liked to try new ways of farming,
and he planted new kinds of crops. He
sold the crops and saw that they were shipped.
He wrote about all of this in a book.

Besides looking after the farms,
Washington had to look after his people.
They lived on his farms and worked for him.

Washington still served Virginia too.
He helped to make the laws for the colony.

As time went on, trouble began between the American colonies and England.

More and more, people in the colonies felt they were Americans, not Englishmen.

"We want to buy and sell goods wherever we can, not just in England," they said.

"We do not want to be taxed by England. We want to make our own laws."

Some of the Americans would not obey the English laws.

The English king sent soldiers to make the Americans obey his laws.

Many people in Virginia and the other colonies wanted to be free of England.

Americans knew that if they wanted their freedom, they must fight for it. So war began with England.

America needed a general to lead the army.

Men said, "We need a leader who is brave and wise. We need a leader who can train an army.

We need a man who will never give up until freedom is won."

They chose George Washington.

Washington wanted to do all he could for his country.

He was not sure he was the best leader for the army. But when they chose him, he said:

"I will do my best."

The American soldiers were proud of
their general.

"He looks like a general," they said.
"And he knows how to fight."

Washington worked to make an army out
of the farm boys. He had to train the men.
He had to work very hard to get food and
clothing and guns for them.

During one winter at Valley Forge, the
soldiers were sick and hungry. Many of
them had no shoes.

The American soldiers won some battles, but they lost many more than they won. Still Washington never gave up. After eight long, hard years, the war for freedom was won.

General Washington was very happy that he could go back to Mount Vernon. But soon his country called him to serve again. He was elected the first president of the United States of America.

His trip to New York City to take the
office of president was like a long, long
parade. At every town people waved flags
and cheered for George Washington.

They threw flowers before his horse's feet.

Being the first president of the United
States was a very hard job. It was not only
a new country, but it had a new kind of
government—government not by a king, but
by the people. Would this new kind of
government work?

Just as he led the army in the long,
hard years of the war, Washington now worked
to build the new country. He made the new
government work, and he made the country strong.

After eight years as president, he went
back to Mount Vernon. How happy he was to
be just Farmer Washington again!

For three more years he enjoyed his life as a farmer and planter.

When he died, the whole country was sad. One man said what the people of America thought of George Washington:

"First in war, first in peace, and first in the hearts of his countrymen."

GEORGE WASHINGTON

Reading Level: Level Three. *George Washington* has a total vocabulary of 378 words. It has been tested in third grade classes, where it was read with ease.

Uses of This Book: An excellent introduction to history. Through this biography of our first president, children in the primary grades will gain an appreciation of why we honor George Washington as the "father of his country."

Word List

5 when	to	old	survey(ing)(ed)	hard
George('s)	over	died	said	work(ing)(ed)
Washington	fields	after	surveyor(s)	walk
was	**6** some	that	what	for
a	day(s)	often	is	miles
boy(s)	rode	stay(ed)(ing)	asked	rain
he	school	at	who	cold
lived(ing)	little	Mount	measure(s)	mud
on	cabin	Vernon	land(s)	could
farm(s)(ing)(er)	later	home	buy	carry
in	went	of	must	make
Virginia	better	Lawrence('s)	be	maps
his	there	were	so	come
father('s)	learn(ed)	parties	will	need(ed)
had	more	friend(s)	know(s)	began
pigs	about	tall	where	**10** sixteen
and	writing	strong	begin(s)	trip(s)
cows	arithmetic	good-looking	ends	with
geese	but	they	maybe	party
chickens	did	treated	I	wilderness
horse(s)('s)	not	him	can	belonged
too	go	man('s)	thought	slept
like(d)	very	**8** one	near(ly)	tent
the	much	mother('s)	fifteen	or
best	from	found	see	under
own	brother(s)	tools	would	stars
pony	manners	long	town	shot
Whitefoot	watching	chain	sir	wild
always	people	those	you	turkeys
good(s)	**7** eleven	are	teach	cooked
ride(r)	year(s)	your	me	meat

fire	take	mean **19**	added **19**	until
saw	got	trouble	new	chose
trapper(s)	just	between	rooms	sure
trader(s)	seventeen	England	house	my
night(s)	proud	France	furnishings **24**	food **24**
an	now	American(s)	married	clothing
Indian(s)(s')	six	colonies	Martha	guns
war	feet	English	Custis	during
camped	big	king	busy	Valley
book	no	sent	happy	Forge
it	than	governor	made	sick
wrote	men	rule	plans	hungry
down	trusted	each	plowing	shoes
dance(r)	born	Europe	plant(ing)(ed)(er) **25**	battles **25**
clear	lead(er)	both	harvesting	lost
large **14**	as	countries **20**	try	gave
circle	country	claimed	kind(s)	eight
great	its	America	crops	called
middle	rivers	order(ed)	sold	again
then	rich	out	shipped	elected
sit	love	message	this	first
around	serve(d)	far	besides	president
speaker	twenty-one	away	look(ing)(s)	United
tell(s)	became	never	helped	States
them	major	gone	laws **26**	New York **26**
how	army	adventure **21**	felt	City
jumps	still **15**	want(ed)	Englishmen	office
up **15**	took **17**	guide	we	parade
runs	into	winter	sell	every
ring	places **18**	back **18**	wherever	waved
rest	talked	making	do	flags
next **12**	sat	soon	taxed	cheered
cousin(s)	French	soldier(s)	by	threw
time	coming	fought	our	flowers
hunting	Canada	drive **22**	obey	before
playing	yes	seven	many **27**	only **27**
games	they're	won	free	governmen(t)
everyone	build(ing)	all	if	three **29**
hear	fort(s)	their	freedom	enjoyed
county **13**	Lake	colonel	fight	life
pass(ed)	Erie	led	general	whole
test	heard **16**	colony	brave	sad
get	other	stop	wise	peace
job	knew	being	train	hearts
way(s)			give	countryme(n)

The Follett BEGINNING-TO-READ Books

Purpose of the Beginning-to-Read Books: To provide easy-to-read materials that will appeal to the interests of primary children. Careful attention is given to vocabulary load and sentence length, but the first criterion is interest to children.

Reading Levels: These books are written at three reading levels, indicated by one, two, or three dots beneath the *Beginning-to-Read* symbol on the back cover. *Level One* books can be read by first grade children in the last half of the school year. As children increase their reading ability they will be able to enjoy *Level Two* books. And as they grow further in their reading ability they will progress to *Level Three* books. Some first grade children will read *Level Two* and *Level Three* books. Many third graders, and even some fourth graders, will read and enjoy *Level One* and *Level Two* books, as well as *Level Three* books. The range of interest of *Beginning-to-Read* books stretches far beyond their reading level.

Use of the Beginning-to-Read Books: Because of their high interest and readability, these books are ideal for independent reading by primary children—at school, in the library, and at home. The books may also be incorporated into the basic reading program to develop children's interests, expand their vocabularies, and improve word-attack skills. It has been suggested that they might serve as the foundation for a skillfully directed reading program. Many *Beginning-to-Read* books correlate with the social studies, science, and other subject fields. All will help children grow in the language arts. Children will read the *Beginning-to-Read* books with confidence, with success, and with real enjoyment.

1298